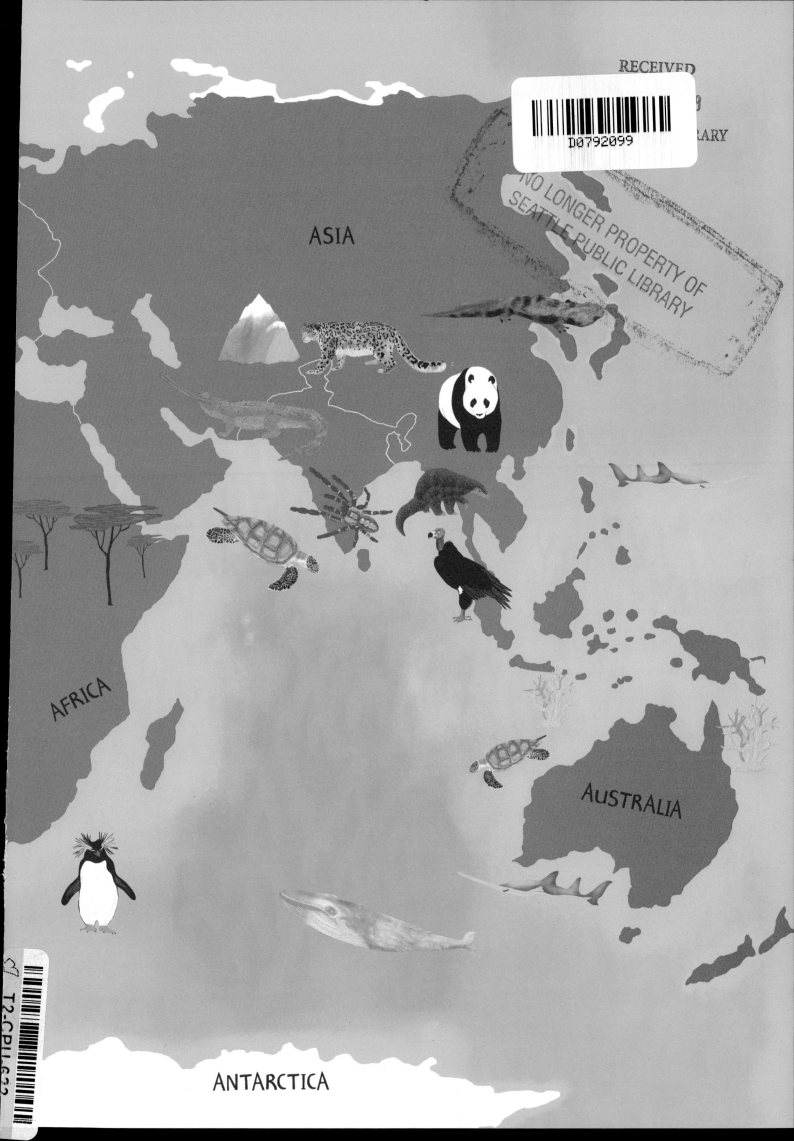

ASIA

AFRICA

AUSTRALIA

ANTARCTICA

For my friend Jeff, who gave me my first job
campaigning for endangered species
at Greenpeace many years ago.—C. B.

For Will, Ella, Mia, and Frank the dog.
It's wonderful sharing this incredible planet with you—A. W.

ACKNOWLEDGMENTS

The author, illustrator, and publishers would like to thank
the following people for their help and advice:

PATRICK CAMPBELL, senior curator, Reptiles, Natural History Museum, London, UK

JEFF CANIN, formerly Greenpeace International sea turtle campaigner

DR. DEAN GRUBBS, associate director of research,
Florida State University Coastal and Marine Laboratory, St. Teresa, FL

CRAIG HILTON-TAYLOR, head, Red List Unit, Global Species Programme,
International Union for Conservation of Nature (IUCN), Cambridge, UK

JEFFREY LANG, professor emeritus, Biology, University of North Dakota, Grand Forks, ND

LORNA LAWSON, head of programmes content, World Wildlife Fund, UK

DR. NISHA OWEN, programme manager, EDGE of Existence, Zoological Society of London, UK

DR. JEFF STREICHER, curator, Amphibians, Natural History Museum, London, UK

Published by Charlesbridge
85 Main Street
Watertown, MA 02472
(617) 926-0329
www.charlesbridge.com

First published in Great Britain in 2018 by Otter-Barry Books,
Little Orchard, Burley Gate, Hereford, HR1 3QS, United Kingdom
www.otterbarrybooks.com

Printed in China
(hc) 10 9 8 7 6 5 4 3 2 1

Library of Congress Cataloging-in-Publication Data
Names: Barr, Catherine, 1965– , author. |
Wilson, Anne, 1974– illustrator.
Title: Red alert! : endangered animals around the world /
written by Catherine Barr; illustrated by Anne Wilson.
Description: First US edition. | Watertown : Charlesbridge, 2017.
Identifiers: LCCN 2017012449 (print) | LCCN 2017048702 (ebook) |
ISBN 9781632897312 (ebook) | ISBN 9781632897329 (ebook pdf) |
ISBN 9781580898393 (reinforced for library use)
Subjects: LCSH: Endangered species—Juvenile literature.
| Wildlife conservation—Study and teaching—
Activity programs—Juvenile literature.
| International Union for Conservation of Nature.
Classification: LCC QL83 (ebook) | LCC QL83 .B367 2017 (print) |
DDC 591.68—dc23
LC record available at https://lccn.loc.gov/2017012449

Illustrations done in mixed media and digital
Display type set in Mr Dodo by Hipopotam Studio
Text type set in Helenita by RodrigoTypo
Printed by Toppan Leefung (Hong Kong) Limited,
in Dongguan, Guangdong, China
Production supervision by Brian G. Walker
Designed by Sarah Richards Taylor

RED ALERT!

Endangered Animals Around the World

Catherine Barr

Illustrated by
Anne Wilson

ini Charlesbridge

"The International Union for Conservation of Nature (IUCN) Red List tells us where we urgently need to do something to prevent the despoliation of this world. It is a great agenda for the work of conservationists."

—Sir David Attenborough,
filmmaker and naturalist known for
the acclaimed *Life on Earth* series

Around the world scientists are collecting stories, facts, and figures that help us understand and care for life on Earth. Some of these scientists work together to maintain a list of endangered animals, plants, and fungi. It is known as the Red List.

The list is red—the color that indicates an emergency— because many of the 80,000 species investigated so far are in danger of disappearing. The information gathered for the Red List is used to help save endangered species.

The Red List team evaluates each animal on the list and assigns it a category. You'll see some of the categories mentioned in this book.

Extinct
Extinct in the Wild
Critically Endangered
Endangered
Vulnerable
Near Threatened
Least Concern

SO LET'S GET STARTED...

Pick a place, then choose a favorite creature, discover its story, and find out how to help to save it.

PICK A PLACE

deserts

forests

mountains

grasslands

rivers

oceans

Pick a place to explore.
Then turn the page to choose a
rare creature that lives there.

CHOOSE A CREATURE

mountains

grasslands

deserts

oceans

forests

rivers

page 28

page 30

page 32

page 36

page 34

page 40

page 24

page 26

page 22

page 14

page 18

page 12

page 38

Choose a creature that lives in the place you chose. Then go to its page to discover its story.

page 20

page 16

Meet the
BLUE WHALE

mammal
Balaenoptera musculus

A Shadowy Story

The blue whale is the biggest animal on Earth. From a boat, whale watchers catch only a blurred shadow as it disappears into deeper water. It is singing songs that echo loudly for miles around its vast ocean home, unheard by humans.

FACTS

➡ The blue whale swims in oceans all around the world, except the Arctic.

➡ Its song is louder than a jet engine during takeoff.

➡ It has the biggest babies on Earth, and its arteries are so big that a human toddler could crawl inside them.

➡ Killing blue whales was banned by the International Whaling Commission in 1966.

Whales were once at home on land. But millions of years ago, their legs became fins, and they returned to the sea, where all life began. But this streamlined ocean giant has been hunted to the edge of extinction. Today whale-watching tourists are lucky if they spot one at all.

DANGER!

Listed as endangered on the IUCN Red List.

⚠ Accidentally hit by ships

⚠ Gets tangled in fishing nets while migrating

⚠ Overfished food source (tiny shrimp called krill)

Go to page 43 to find out how to help the blue whale.

Meet the
SUNDA PANGOLIN

mammal
Manis javanica

A Shy Story

The most hunted animal in the world rolls up into a ball, covering its head with its front legs. It is scared. But this one is lucky, because it is rescued by a wildlife ranger from hunters who want its meat and scales.

FACTS

➡ The Sunda pangolin lives in grasslands and forests across Southeast Asia.

➡ Its tongue is longer than its body.

➡ Its name comes from the Malay word *pengguling*, which means "one that rolls up."

➡ It is one of the few mammals that is completely covered in scales.

The Sunda pangolin is shy and secretive. It shuffles around at night, sniffing out termites and ants to lap up with its long sticky tongue. Its scales protect it from predators such as tigers. But human hunters can pick it up when it rolls into a ball. The ranger will tell people the pangolin's story. With luck it can return to the wild. Pangolins struggle to survive away from their natural home.

DANGER!

Listed as critically endangered on the IUCN Red List.

⚠ Hunted for its meat and scales

⚠ Limited conservation funding because it is a lesser-known animal

⚠ Forest habitat threatened by human activities

Go to page 43 to find out how to help the Sunda pangolin.

PANAMANIAN GOLDEN FROG

Amphibian
Atelopus zeteki

An Unlucky Story

Leaping across rocks beneath rushing water, a slippery yellow frog escapes a zookeeper's grasp. The zookeeper wears gloves to protect himself from the frog's poisonous skin, which it uses to escape from predators. The frog is caught and taken to a "frog hotel" to save it from a mysterious disease that is sweeping through the forest. It can breed safely in captivity.

FACTS

➡ The signals the frog uses are highly unusual in amphibians.

➡ Its skin is poisonous to humans who touch it.

➡ The Panamanian golden frog lives in the mountainous cloud forests of Panama in Central America.

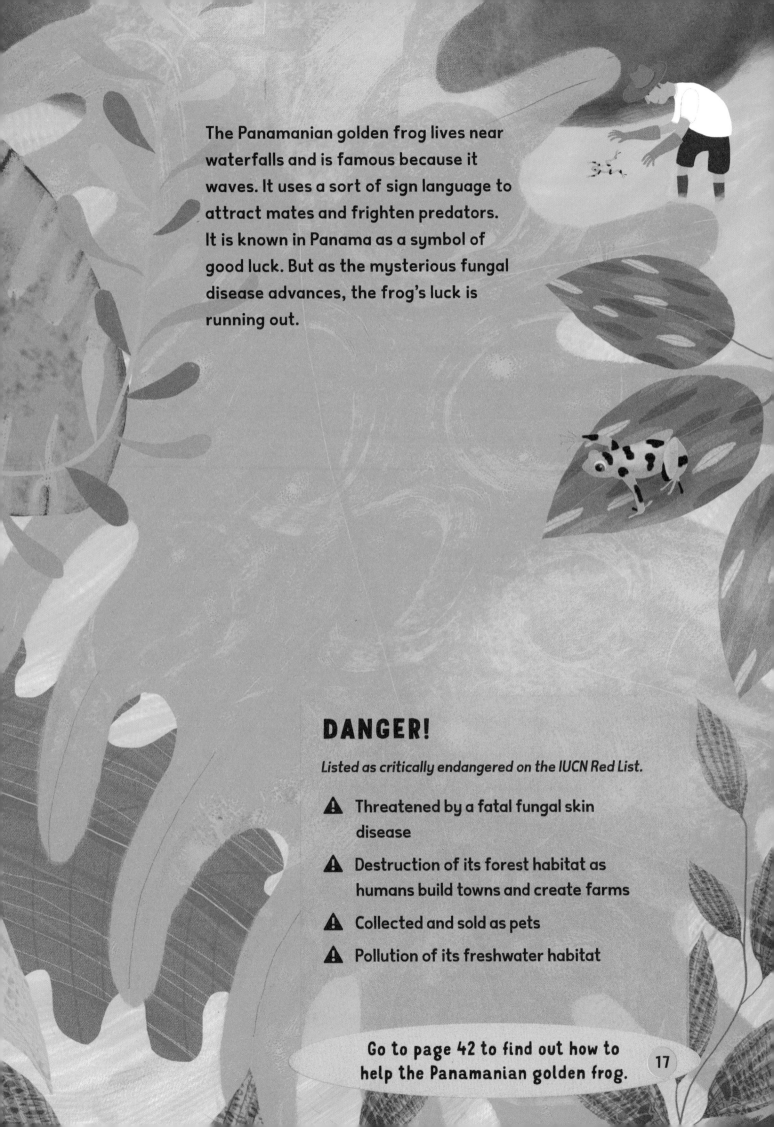

The Panamanian golden frog lives near waterfalls and is famous because it waves. It uses a sort of sign language to attract mates and frighten predators. It is known in Panama as a symbol of good luck. But as the mysterious fungal disease advances, the frog's luck is running out.

DANGER!

Listed as critically endangered on the IUCN Red List.

⚠ Threatened by a fatal fungal skin disease

⚠ Destruction of its forest habitat as humans build towns and create farms

⚠ Collected and sold as pets

⚠ Pollution of its freshwater habitat

Go to page 42 to find out how to help the Panamanian golden frog.

Meet the
NORTHERN ROCKHOPPER PENGUIN

bird
Eudyptes moseleyi

A Sketchy Story

A bird with extraordinary eyebrows is hopping from rock to rock. A wildlife artist is sketching the northern rockhopper penguin. The penguin seems angry—a bigger bird is trying to steal its eggs.

FACTS

➡ Lives near the South Atlantic and Indian Oceans.

➡ Unlike other penguins, it jumps rather than waddles.

➡ It can dive up to 325 feet (100 meters) deep.

DANGER!

Listed as endangered on the IUCN Red List.

⚠ Gets caught in fishing gear

⚠ Illegal collection of its eggs

⚠ Overfished food source (squid and krill)

Go to page 42 to find out how to help the northern rockhopper penguin.

Living in huge colonies, these penguins return to nest with the same partner each year. But the wild population of this quirky bird has diminished over the past thirty years. The artist wants to capture this one's personality.

A Nosy Story

Unable to lift its belly off the sand like other crocodiles, the enormous gharial, or fish-eating crocodile, shuffles up the river bank. It has razor-sharp teeth and a lump on the end of its nose. A camera clicks as a photographer captures an image of this strange-looking reptile.

FACTS

➡ Gharials live in large rivers in India and Nepal.

➡ Males grow to almost twenty feet (six meters) long.

➡ Their snout gets longer and thinner as they get older.

➡ The lump on the male's nose is called a *ghara*.

In fast-flowing water, these crocodiles use their slender nose to sneak up on fish. Only males have a lump on their nose, which they use to make a sound to attract females. The photographer focuses on the animal. He wants local children to see the rare river creature that lives so close to their school.

DANGER!

Listed as critically endangered on the IUCN Red List.

⚠ Gets tangled in fishing nets

⚠ Too little water in its river habitat before rainy season

⚠ River pollution and damming by humans

Go to page 43 to find out how to help the gharial.

A Meaty Story

Vultures are circling above a pile of dead animals while a man watches from his truck. He has dumped fresh waste meat for the huge birds. Red-headed vultures eat the carrion, leaving a pile of clean bones. This helps stop disease.

Where wild food is scarce, red-headed vultures feed on dead livestock. But a certain medicine given to cattle makes their meat poisonous to vultures. These giant birds are dying as they feed on domestic animals. The truck driver is glad to help these birds by bringing them a healthy "vulture restaurant."

DANGER!

Listed as critically endangered on the IUCN Red List.

⚠ Poisoned by medicine used to treat livestock in some countries

⚠ Poisoned by chemicals used to catch fish and birds at watering holes

⚠ Loses nesting habitat because tall trees are cut for firewood

Go to page 42 to find out how to help the red-headed vulture.

Meet the
RED-HEADED VULTURE

bird
Sarcogyps calvus

FACTS

➡ The red-headed vulture lives in wooded hills and dry forests across India and Southeast Asia.

➡ It helps get rid of dead animals that could spread disease to humans and other animals.

➡ Males and females both cartwheel through the air to attract a mate.

➡ Females usually lay only one egg per year.

Meet the
CHINESE GIANT SALAMANDER

amphibian
Andrias davidianus

A Slippery Story

The ancestors of this huge slimy creature once swam with dinosaurs. This one lies still in a cool mountain lake. It's dusk, and the largest amphibian in the world is hiding. But before the Chinese giant salamander can ambush its prey, it is surprised by visiting scientists.

FACTS

➡ The Chinese giant salamander lives in high rocky mountain streams and some lakes in China.

➡ It breathes through its skin.

➡ In Chinese it is often called "infant fish" because it makes a whining, crying sound.

➡ It is the largest of all living amphibians, growing to almost six feet (1.8 meters) long.

DANGER!

Listed as critically endangered on the IUCN Red List.

⚠ Hunted for its meat, which some consider a delicacy

⚠ Habitat threatened as trees are cut and soil creates silt in rivers

⚠ River pollution by farming chemicals

Go to page 43 to find out how to help the Chinese giant salamander.

Sticky goo seeps from the salamander's wrinkled skin when it is scared. The substance keeps it safe from non-human predators. But it is hunted by humans for meat, and thousands are farmed to provide expensive meals. Once the scientists have measured it, this wild one slips back to safety, finding crabs, fish, and frogs for its supper.

A Stealthy Story

Dawn breaks as a snow leopard's soft gray eyes scan the snow. It flicks its tail as a cameraman stares down his lens at one of the world's rarest big cats. The leopard pads softly into focus.

This mountain cat cannot roar, and it lives alone. To catch prey, it must spring into action—leaping across ledges to bring down wild sheep and goats. Because the snow leopard is so difficult to find, the cameraman, stiff with cold, is proud to have finally gotten a photograph of the secretive cat.

FACTS

➡ The snow leopard lives in the steep, rocky mountains of twelve countries in Central Asia.

➡ It is sometimes called "ghost of the mountains" because it is shy and difficult to find.

➡ It wraps its long thick tail around itself like a scarf and can jump like an acrobat.

➡ It can hiss, purr, and make a puffing *chuff* noise.

DANGER!

Changed from endangered to vulnerable on the IUCN Red List due to new population estimates, but action is still needed.

⚠ Illegally hunted for its fluffy white coat

⚠ Disappearance of its habitat and prey as domestic animals graze bigger areas

⚠ Conflict with humans as hungry snow leopards steal livestock

Go to page 43 to find out how to help the snow leopard.

A Slinky Story

Slithering from its dusty burrow at sunset, this snake has just woken up. It stretches sleepily across a path. As a woman wanders past, she almost steps on its camouflaged body. If the snake had been able to rattle, the woman might have noticed it.

The Santa Catalina rattlesnake is the only rattlesnake in the world without a rattle. Each time this snake sheds its skin, the segment that would create a rattle falls off rather than staying at the end of its tail like on other rattlesnakes. Scientists believe that the snake evolved for stealth, so it can slink silently toward prey. The young tourist walks on, unaware of her close encounter with this quiet, venomous little snake.

FACTS

➡ The Santa Catalina rattlesnake lives only on Isla Santa Catalina Island off the coast of Mexico.

➡ It is a stealthy hunter and is good at slithering up trees.

➡ It has a heat-sensing "pit" between its eyes, which helps it find warm-blooded prey.

DANGER!

Listed as critically endangered on the IUCN Red List.

⚠ Hunted and eaten by feral cats

⚠ Caught illegally and sold as pets

⚠ Limited conservation funding because of a lack of interest in snakes

Go to page 42 to find out how to help the Santa Catalina rattlesnake.

29

Meet the
HAWKSBILL SEA TURTLE

reptile
Eretmochelys imbricata

An Ancient Story

Leaving a trail like tire tracks, the hawksbill sea turtle crawls up the beach to nest after an exhausting journey. It has crossed the ocean and is here at last to lay eggs. The eggs fall like soft balls into a hole in the sand as a scientist counts them.

A tropical night breeze brushes over the turtle. It will not wait to see the young hatch and scamper toward the ocean. Many of the babies will be grabbed by gulls, and few will survive. The scientist counts as the last egg drops from the weary mother turtle. The scientist writes "100" in her notes.

DANGER!

Listed as critically endangered on the IUCN Red List.

⚠ Hunted for its shell and eggs

⚠ Beach and coral reef habitats threatened by human activity and tourism

⚠ Climate change killing coral reef food sources

⚠ Gets caught in fishing gear

Go to page 43 to find out how to help the hawksbill sea turtle.

FACTS

➡ The hawksbill sea turtle is mostly found in the warm waters of the Atlantic, Indian, and Pacific Oceans.

➡ It is called "hawksbill" because of its narrow, sharp beak.

➡ It helps keep coral reefs healthy by grazing on sponges and exposing food and shelter for other reef animals.

A Pale Story

Tipping over the edge of the dive boat, a snorkeler tumbles into the tropical water. She is excited to see a ray swim by. But then she looks sadly at the spiky carpet of white coral all around her—it is mostly dead.

Coral reefs are the "rain forests of the sea" and are supposed to be full of color and life. Orange, purple, and pink staghorn corals help create reefs in shallow waters, providing food and shelter to plants and other animals. But as climate change warms the oceans, the bright colors are fading because corals are dying. The snorkeler searches for fish in this area, but not many live here anymore.

FACTS

➡ Staghorn coral is found in the Caribbean Sea, parts of the Gulf of Mexico, in the waters of Southeast Asia, and on the Australian Great Barrier Reef.

➡ This coral is important in creating reefs, which support a quarter of all marine life.

➡ Coral is an animal—it doesn't make its own food.

DANGER!

Listed as critically endangered on the IUCN Red List.

⚠ Climate change makes oceans too warm

⚠ Destroyed by storms and extreme weather, also related to climate change

⚠ Killed by coral disease

⚠ Harmed by marine pollution

Go to page 42 to find out how to help staghorn coral.

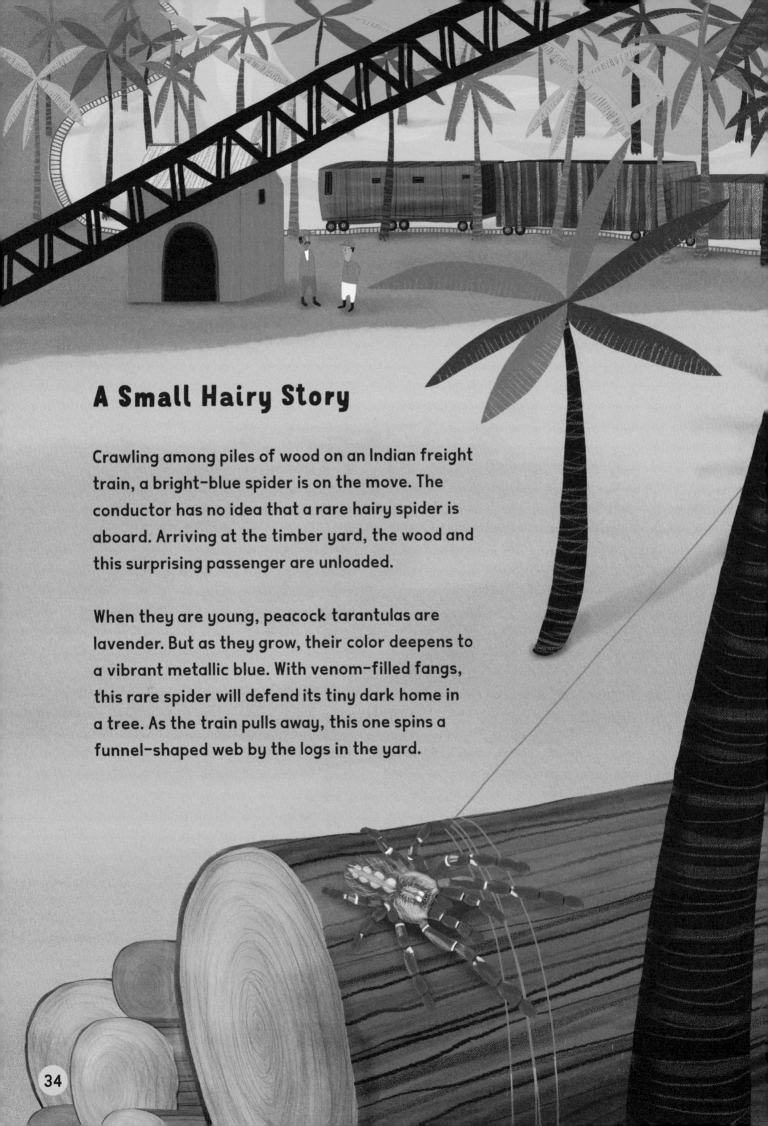

A Small Hairy Story

Crawling among piles of wood on an Indian freight train, a bright-blue spider is on the move. The conductor has no idea that a rare hairy spider is aboard. Arriving at the timber yard, the wood and this surprising passenger are unloaded.

When they are young, peacock tarantulas are lavender. But as they grow, their color deepens to a vibrant metallic blue. With venom-filled fangs, this rare spider will defend its tiny dark home in a tree. As the train pulls away, this one spins a funnel-shaped web by the logs in the yard.

FACTS

➡ The peacock tarantula lives in a small area of forest in central southern India.

➡ It is very aggressive, and its venom can cause humans a lot of pain.

➡ When it molts, it lies on its back with its legs in the air and looks like it is dead.

➡ Females live for about twelve years—up to four times longer than males.

DANGER!

Listed as critically endangered on the IUCN Red List.

⚠ Human destruction of its forest habitat

⚠ Overharvesting of firewood from its forest habitat

Go to page 42 to find out how to help the peacock tarantula.

35

A Sharp Story

This largetooth sawfish's bizarre snout is hopelessly tangled in a fishing net. It was looking for food on the muddy seafloor when it got stuck. But the fishermen in the boat above are unaware of the struggle of the huge shark-like ray far below the surface.

Using its strange saw, this gigantic ray defends itself from sharks and other predators when it hunts at night. But the saw can also get it into trouble. The fishermen will cut it free when they find it in the net.

FACTS

➡ The largetooth sawfish lives in fresh and marine waters, particularly around Australia.

➡ It can live up to eighty years.

➡ Its mouth is under the front part of its body and is full of tiny teeth.

➡ Newborn pups have fully formed saws covered in sheaths that eventually disintegrate and fall off.

DANGER!

Listed as critically endangered on the IUCN Red List.

⚠ Easily trapped in fishing gear

⚠ Hunted for its saw nose, meat, skin (for leather), and fins (for soup)

⚠ Loss of habitat due to coastal development

Go to page 43 to find out how to help the largetooth sawfish.

Meet the
BONOBO

mammal
Pan paniscus

A Love Story

A group of bonobos are cuddling one another by the river, deep in the jungle. Treading carefully on the forest floor, a local park ranger creeps close enough to count these rare apes.

Like chimpanzees, bonobos are close relatives of humans. But they are different from chimps, which are led by males and can be violent or aggressive. Bonobos are led by females and work out problems with physical affection. They make close friendships and spend time together in large groups. Watching baby bonobos playing by the water, the ranger is reminded of her own children at home.

FACTS

➡ The bonobo lives in forests near rivers only in the Democratic Republic of the Congo in Africa.

➡ It was the last of the big apes to be discovered.

➡ Like chimpanzees, female bonobos give birth every five to six years.

➡ The bonobo is mostly vegetarian, with more than half its diet made up of fruit.

DANGER!

Listed as endangered on the IUCN Red List.

⚠ Poached for meat

⚠ Forest habitat cut down to grow crops

⚠ Wars and other human fighting surround its habitat

Go to page 43 to find out how to help the bonobo.

Meet the
GIANT PANDA

mammal
Ailuropoda melanoleuca

A Good-News Story

Giant highways cut through the thick bamboo forests that are home to giant pandas. Pandas are shy, and finding a mate can be difficult. Forests are being divided by roads and cut down for farmland. But in these remote places, workers are now digging tunnels so the bears can safely cross roads.

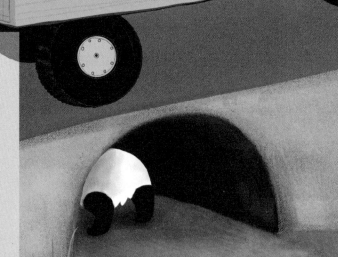

DANGER!

Changed from endangered to vulnerable on the IUCN Red List due to conservation efforts, but action is still needed.

⚠ Bamboo forests cut down for farmland

⚠ Struggles to find a mate in isolated forests

⚠ Starvation because bamboo plants blossom and then die about every sixty years

Go to page 43 to find out how to help the giant panda.

FACTS

➡ Giant pandas do everything slowly because bamboo doesn't provide much nutrition.

➡ The giant panda lives in bamboo forests in the mountains of Western China.

➡ If a panda has two cubs, it will usually take care of only one of them.

Pandas eat only bamboo, so they are fussy about where they live. Giant pandas are often isolated. Panda tunnels help bears find one another. This creates new hope for these solitary animals.

YOU CAN HELP!

Find out how to help your favorite creature survive.

Then turn to page 8 to pick another place, then to page 10 to choose another animal, and do it again!

The URLs listed here were accurate at the time of publication, but websites often change. If a URL doesn't work, you can use the internet to find more information.

PEACOCK TARANTULA

Plant a tree to help forest habitats.

http://www.earthday.org /campaigns/reforestation /help-us-plant-trees

Do

Join a wildlife club or charity that helps endangered species.

SANTA CATALINA RATTLESNAKE

Read about conservation efforts to protect all types of snakes.

http://www.snakeconservation.org

Ask

Inspire your parents, teachers, and friends to join conservation efforts.

NORTHERN ROCKHOPPER PENGUIN

Adopt a penguin (for a fee) and receive updates while helping conservation efforts.

http://www.penguins.cl /rockhopper-penguins.htm

PANAMANIAN GOLDEN FROG

Read about the Maryland Zoo, the first to successfully breed these frogs in captivity.

http://www.marylandzoo.org /animals-conservation /amphibians/panamanian-golden-frog/

Save

Raise money by starting a penny jar at school or having a bake sale.

STAGHORN CORAL

Download the Coral Reef Resource Pack for your teacher.

http://www.edgeofexistence.org /edgeucation/

RED-HEADED VULTURE

Use IUCN's matching game, choose an animal, and receive updates about how it's doing.

http://support.iucnredlist.org /matching-game

BLUE WHALE

Save whales from fishing gear by learning more about sustainable seafood.
http://ocean.si.edu/sustainable-seafood

GHARIAL

Research zoo programs that help breed gharials in captivity.
http://www.gharialconservation alliance.org/?page_id=229

Care

Fall in love with an endangered animal and find out more about how to help it.

LARGETOOTH SAWFISH

Share a sawfish infographic with your class.
http://www.dulvy.com/uploads /2/1/0/4/21048414/sawfish _infographicv2_copy.pdf

CHINESE GIANT SALAMANDER

Become a Wildlife Champion.
http://edgeofexistence.org/champions

Learn

Do some digging by reading a book, looking online, or talking to an expert.

GIANT PANDA

Read and find out how to help.
http://www.worldwildlife.org /species/giant-panda

SNOW LEOPARD

Sign up for a newsletter.
http://www.snowleopard.org

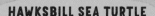

Share

Spread the word by making a poster or writing a poem about an animal.

HAWKSBILL SEA TURTLE

Read about saving these turtles, and sign up to receive a newsletter.
http://www.wicked adventures.com/turtle -conservation-camp

SUNDA PANGOLIN

Read about saving pangolins.
http://www.savepangolins.org

BONOBO

Explore an interactive map to learn about where bonobos live.
http://www.bonobo.org /peace-forest-map

THE STORY OF THE IUCN RED LIST

⚠ In 1933, an American conservationist named John C. Phillips was worried about the number of rare animals, plants, and fungi threatened with extinction, so he began to make a list.

⚠ The list was adopted by a big new international organization called the International Union for Conservation of Nature (IUCN), and in 1964 it became the IUCN Red List, a global list of rare animals, plants, and fungi.

⚠ IUCN frequently published Red Data Books about mammals, birds, reptiles, amphibians, flowering plants, and freshwater fish. And *The Red Book—Wildlife in Danger* was published in 1969.

⚠ The IUCN's Amazing Species campaign raises awareness about the Red List, which includes 88,000 species.

⚠ The IUCN Red List is updated every year and aims to collect data about 160,000 species by 2020. (There are 8.7 million known species on Earth!)

⚠ The IUCN Red List has a goal to "provide information and analyses on the status, trends, and threats to species to inform and catalyze action for biodiversity conservation."

⚠ *Homo sapiens*, or humans, were assessed in 2008 and added to the list under the category "least concern."

To find out more, visit http://www.iucnredlist.org.

Please note that IUCN Red List status of the fifteen creatures in this book was accurate at the time of publication.

The red creatures below are the ones in this book.
The numbered creatures on this page are sixty others on the Red List.

1. Burmese roofed turtle
2. aye-aye
3. pygmy raccoon
4. olm
5. puma
6. porbeagle
7. orangutan
8. Hector's dolphin
9. southern three-banded armadillo
10. green humphead parrotfish
11. western gorilla
12. Galápagos sea lion
13. brown spider monkey
14. polar bear
15. Sir David's long-beaked echidna
16. whale shark
17. far eastern curlew
18. golden-rumped sengi
19. moscardón
20. sperm whale

21. desert rain frog
22. Sumatran rhinoceros
23. Sumatran tiger
24. pygmy hippopotamus
25. Jerdon's courser
26. pink river dolphin
27. Tarzan's chameleon
28. marvelous spatuletail hummingbird
29. Darwin's frog
30. rapa fruit-dove
31. steppe eagle
32. okapi
33. volcano rabbit
34. Lord Howe Island stick insect
35. angel shark
36. Malay tapir
37. proboscis monkey
38. kakapo
39. giant devil ray
40. red wolf

41. northern brown kiwi
42. addax
43. northern quoll
44. Cuban greater funnel-eared bat
45. Asian elephant
46. ring-tailed lemur
47. banded cotinga
48. American burying beetle
49. lion-tailed macaque
50. hyacinth macaw
51. sun bear
52. black rhinoceros
53. yellow-eared parrot
54. pygmy three-toed sloth
55. Devil's Hole pupfish
56. grey-breasted parakeet
57. Przewalski's horse
58. red panda
59. hammerhead shark
60. Bahia tapaculo